LOVE AND PAIN

LOVE AND PAIN

By Walter Brim

Dedication

I want to dedicate this book to my best friend and wife, Genise. I thank God for her support and her help and for believing in me. I also thank my sons Sherrod and Devon, and grandson Braylen Brim, for their support. Most importantly, I thank God for inspiring me to write this book.

CONTENTS

CHAPTER 1

WHAT IS MARRIAGE?

Marriage is a formal union; a social and legal contract between two individuals that unites them legally, economically, and emotionally. The contractual marriage agreement usually implies that the couple now has legal obligations to each other throughout their lives, except for the case of divorce. As such, sexual relations is a phenomenon that is only legitimate within marriage.

Traditionally, marriage is often seen to play a key role in the preservation of morals and civilization. The first marriage occurred in Genesis; the book of beginnings. And the Lord God formed man from the dust of the ground, and breathed life into his nostrils the breath of life; and man became a living being" (Genesis 2:7).

Though Adam lived in a beautiful and perfect World, it had one exception. Adam was alone. The world was full of animals of every kind, and God allowed Adam to name them all (verse 19). Adam learned how different he was from all the animals on Earth. He was made in God's "image." By the time Adam finished naming the animals, he was likely very aware of how alone he was.

And the Lord God said, 'It is not good that man should be alone; I will make him a helper comparable to him'" (verse 18). For this course, God took one of Adam's ribs and formed a perfect complement—a woman.

She was the ideal companion— he could share his deepest thoughts and desires with her, and just as important, he could build and raise a family with her. After God presented His newest creation to Adam, the Bible tells us, "Therefore, a man shall leave his father and mother and be joined to his wife, and they shall become one flesh" (verse 24). The first marriage began when Adam and Eve became man and wife. Marriage was to be an inseparable union. The fact that God created Eve from one of Adam's ribs seems to reflect the permanent and intimate connection that was always to be between them. They shared some of the same substance, and they were to share their lives from that point on. They created a family unit were they enjoyed deep conversations, quiet moments, difficulties and stress, and experienced the kind of intimate, physical relationship that God intended for couples alone.

The bible shows Adam and Eve living out their lives with each other and having children. For some generations, it appears their children followed their example; marrying, raising children and watching their children grow up to marry and start their own families. Among the 10 Commandments that were written and given to Moses at Mount Sinai, the 7 Commandment clearly stated, "You shall not commit adultery" (Exodus 20:14). God did not want anything or anyone to interfere with the special relationship between a husband and wife. "Then God blessed them, and God said to them, 'Be fruitful and multiply; fill the earth and subdue it; have dominion over the fish of the sea, over the birds of the air, and over every living thing that moves on the earth." God designed marriage to be a lifelong, faithful relationship between one man and one woman. Adam was created first and was initially the only human; however, from one of his ribs, God lovingly formed a woman and presented her to him. They were "one flesh," and she perfectly complemented Adam. Together they formed a whole; they built a family, having and raising children together. Through the words of Jesus Christ, we can see that God's perspective of marriage as a loving, monogamous relationship between one man and one woman has not changed. In the New Testament God reaffirms it and shows how very important fidelity within marriage is. Men and women are different by design, but they were created to complement each other. God intended for children, only through a marriage relationship, to be brought into the world to be raised and taught under the loving, thoughtful care of their mother and father.

Marriage & Love Relationship: A Complete Marriage.

A reality that many people do not seem to be familiar with is the different types of Love. There are four types of love that must always be present for marriage to be complete. The absence of any one of them creates a hole in a relationship. When the four kinds of love are active in your marriage, it'll be more secure.

A Complete Marriage

A marriage relationship is built over time. There are four kinds of "love" needed to make a marriage relationship complete. These include AGAPE, PHILEO, STORGE, and EROS. All are important in marriage.

The greatest of the four types is agape. Agape love is an unconditional love. It persists when the others quit. This love never quits because it comes from God. When a person asks Jesus to come into their heart and be their Lord and Savior, God gives them the Agape kind of love. God is our example. He shows his own agape love toward us. Even while we were still sinners, Christ died for us (Romans 5:8). He likewise commands all husbands to love, agape, their wives as Christ also loved the church and gave himself for her (Ephesians 5:25).

Phileo love is the kind of love that makes agape love enjoyable. Phileo love is having tender affection for another person. Most friendships are built on phileo love. Phileo love is the attraction that draws you to become another's friend. It's one thing to have unconditional love (agape) toward someone you don't like being around because they irritate you. It's quite another thing to unconditionally love someone who is tenderly affectionate (phileo) toward you. The tender affection of phileo love makes the unconditional love of agape enjoyable. It's the joy of the friendship.

Although Phileo is referred to as human love, God the Father, who is not a human, but a Spirit, phileo love Jesus his son and us. Jesus said for the father himself loves, phileo, you because you have loved (phileo) me (John 16:27).

God's desire for the husband and wife is that they show gentleness in love (phileo) to each other while they overlook each other's faults and failures (agape).

Another kind of love needed in a marriage is storge. Storge is a physical show of affection that results from a pure motive. It may be a hug, a kiss, or another expression of affection. On the basis of personality, women are seen to need this kind of love more than men. In marriage, it is important for the man to set aside his needs to meet his wife's main need; affection.

Eros love is also needed to make a marriage work. Eros is the fulfillment of the physical, sexual desire that a man and woman show toward each other. It's when the two become one flesh (Matthew 19:5).

When all the kinds of love operate in a marriage, the marriage is complete. A husband and wife who lay down their life for each other, no matter how many times they both offend themselves or cause each other to have ill feelings, have agape love. They both have tender affection toward each other (phileo love). They enjoy each other's company because they're best friends. Because they enjoy each other so much, they hug, kiss, hold hands and do nice things for their spouse (storge love). Because their hearts are filled with agape, phileo, storge, there is a warm, passionate desire to enjoy each other sexually; Eros. This kind of marriage is God-centered and can deal with any storm that comes its way.

In marriage, the four kinds of love must be guarded equally. Failure of either of the four leaves a hole in the relationship. To show you the significance and impact of this in our relationships, I would share our experience; the result of removing one type of love at a time, so you can see how incomplete the other three are alone.

OUR STORY

This is the story of how I met my wife, Genise. One Friday night, while I went to spend the day with my sister Cora in Daytona Beach, I came across Genise. My sister and I had actually before now decided to go to the Jai-Alai frontons in Daytona. While in Daytona, I told my sister Cora that I was going to check it out and see what numbers came out. As I was walking up the ramp, I saw a beautiful girl working; directing people to their seat. As I approached her, the only thing I could say to her was, "I am going to get you girl, you are mine." Unfortunately, at the time, the company I was working for put me on a 2nd shift work period and as a result, I could not get away. However, I kept thinking about her. One day while in a convenience store in Daytona, we passed each other and greeted "Hi." At first, I did not recognize her, but after we had passed each other, I did. Well, whatever the case, she always stayed on my mind. I went back to her part-time job at the highlight to see if she was there, but they told me that she no longer worked there. Because I met her in the night I didn't get her name, the only thing I actually knew about her, was that she had long hair, was light-skinned and drove a white car. When I went home that night, God spoke to me through a dream. He said, "go to Daytona, drive down Campbell street, the first person you see pull over and ask them if they know a girl with long hair, who is light skinned and drives a white car." Early the next morning, I drove to Daytona to do what God instructed me to do in order to find her. Once I got to Daytona, I drove down Campbell Street and not one person was walking outside at the time. It was 9:00 AM in the morning. However, when I drove down the street a second time, I saw two girls walking and I pulled over to ask them the question. I hesitated. I told God I couldn't ask them a question like that but he said "do it," so I asked, "do you know a girl, long hair, light skinned, who drives a white car." One of the girls replied, "That's my sister." I was excited, so I responded with, "She's your sister? Show me where she lives." The two girls got in my truck, but they did not take me to see her. Instead, they took me to her parents. There, we stayed and talked for about 1 hour. When we were done at, the young ladies got back into my truck and we drove to their sister's apartment. While we drove, I had this raging thought that this might not be the girl I was looking for. So, I decided to hide behind the door to see if she was the one when we got there. However, if she wasn't the one, I won't play it off. I couldn't be disrespectful; I just was not raised that way. We arrived, her sister knocked on the door and when she opened and walked outside, I looked at her, from behind the door, and confirmed she was the right girl. God planned our relationship. We started spending time together, so much so that I spent my weekends in Daytona with her. She had her own apartment, so where to sleep wasn't a bother. However, I slept on her couch to avoid the temptation of sex. Whenever my hormones got out of control, I spent the night at my sister's house in Daytona. Sex had nothing to do with the love that existed in our relationship. We became best of friends and did things together; being around her was fun. We laughed and talked about everything; we really had good chemistry and were very comfortable with each other. She had a beautiful smile, and her dimples always made it better. Our relationship was going great after a few months.

In another dream, God spoke to me and told me she was the one I was meant to marry. He told me to go to a jewelry store and pick out an engagement ring. I did as he instructed. I made plans to take her out to dinner with friends; I proposed at that dinner. Although she said yes, she had just one problem with me; I drank alcohol. She used to tell me that she did not want to marry someone that drank a lot of alcohol because her father was an alcoholic. She did not like my drinking. I had told her I would stop but didn't; I just cut back. However, she just kept praying that God should take away the desire for alcohol from me. I started to drink one beer every other day, but nevertheless; I had a relapse. She just kept on praying. I bought a quart of beer and a few days after that; I got sick due to drinking. After that experience, I had no desire to drink anymore. When she saw that God had removed that desire from me, she agreed for a wedding date. The wedding was set to hold on May 16, 1987, and we began planning for the wedding.

When we eventually got married, we were always very busy in the church.

Tested early in marriage

This is how the devil worked. My test came from a lady that I used to work with. I tried having a relationship with her before I got married, but she turned me down. However, once she heard I was getting married she wanted to talk. One day while I passed by her office, she stopped me and asked, "Walter, do you know men mess around after their first year of marriage?" I replied, "When I get the urge, you would be my first option." I went back to my desk and called Genise; I told her what she asked and what my reply was. Could you believe that this girl wrote down our anniversary date on her calendar? So, when it was my anniversary, she blocked me in the hallways and asked, "Are you ready?" "Ready for what?" I asked. She said she was ready to mess around, that it had been a year. I paused for a moment and asked her, "do you think I am willing to lose my wife for a one-night stand?" "what would happen if I didn't satisfy you, would you come back for me a day later? And how would I be able to look at my wife after cheating on her? How would I be able to hold her with all my heart?" Once again, I went back to my desk and called my wife Genise; I told her exactly what she said and what I replied. Genise had also been approached by guys, but she always told them she was happily married. She did tell me about their approaches. This was the same thing she would have to face if she cheated. How would she hold me knowing she was unfaithful? Was that possible? Would it be possible to hold me with all her heart if she had cheated? Neither of us faulted others for trying to seduce either spouse but we would have to fault ourselves if we fell into the temptation. What does God word say about Satan? He comes to steal, kill and destroy. Satan uses some people to steal joy, happiness and kill relationships. So, always remember the value of what you have at home. Also, you must know and believe that you are a born-again believer in Jesus Christ.

Being tested early in Finance and your Job

Genise and I were so blessed, we got married at such an early age, with excellent jobs. We were also blessed with two sons and could afford to buy our first home in our early twenties. But the job market started to change and I went through about (6) layoffs and (5) plant closures; things got very difficult for us. But Genise and I were blessed not to get in an argument about our finances; we just lived through that rough patch. Jesus Christ took care of us through all of it. For the time of that period, we stayed busy doing the work of God.

The reason we told you the story of how we met and even told you about our financial difficulties and temptations is to let you know that marriage will not be easy. Sometimes we even get on each other's nerves but at the end of the day, we are still best friends. I would not want to spend the rest of my life with any other person. I am still very happy, and in love with my best friend Genise, and on May 2019 we were blessed with 32 years of marriage. What God has joined together let no man put asunder. God put our marriage together, so we got so busy doing his work because we knew that our marriage was founded in God. The point I'm trying to make is, you must be a born again in Jesus Christ to make a marriage work. Without God, it is impossible to deal with everything that comes our way in marriage. We all know that nobody is exempted from trials and temptations, ups and downs, good days and bad days, so it is of utmost importance that you understand who you have at home.

Buy your Wife or girlfriend /Husband or Boyfriend gifts just because?

Do not wait for a holiday to buy a gift for the one you love. Buy a gift just because you want to. Waiting until a holiday to buy a gift might make you feel like you have an obligation do so. I believe couples should always try to keep the excitement in their relationship. I am not suggesting buying a gift all the time; I am only saying, "please do not wait for a holiday to show your love for your spouse." You should show your love every day. You might hear someone say, "My boyfriend never gets me anything, aside from Christmas gifts, valentine day gifts, etc." "I've never gotten a "just because" gift." "Do you buy your spouse gifts 'just because' you want to see a smile on his/her face?"

Decide on a romantic gesture, or a present that fits any upcoming occasion, it'll give you enough time to plan and execute. It would also give you the time you need to express your love.

WHO PICKS WHO?

Whoso findeth a wife findeth a good thing, and obtaineth favour of the Lord.

Proverbs 18:22 King James Version (KJV)

The Bible says that when a man finds a wife, he finds a good thing because he found the woman. However, some women do not want to be with the man that finds them, because they believe he is neither their type nor what they are looking for. I believe that at the beginning of a relationship between a man and a woman, the woman is in control. For example, when a man and woman go to a club to have a wonderful time, they both look around to see who they are attracted to. Five or four men see the same woman and are attracted to her. She finally rejects four men and chooses the man she is attracted to. It does not depend on how each of the men talked to the same woman, the truth is, she has already selected which man she would like to be with before there approach. In another case, five guys can see the same girl and each approach her for a dance. Four-time she is approached, she says she does not want to dance, but finally, she says yes to one of the guys and dances with him. So, who is in control at the beginning of a relationship? Guys, you know what I'm talking about, you can relate to being rejected. Although both women and men can be rejected.

Back to the example, the two spend most of their evening dancing and enjoying themselves. They believe that with this person, it is not about sex but a special connection or chemistry. They both do not want to mess up what they feel by going home with each other. So, she gives him her phone number, at that point; I believe the man is now in control. This is because the woman will be waiting to see if the man will call. If the man does not call, the woman will be devastated and disappointed. However, if both exchange phone numbers, I believe it gives equal grounds for either party to make a move. What if the woman called first? Would she be wrong? It may not be the way it used to be, but in today's society, women are becoming more forward and taking more charge of their life.

In some cases, a woman would wait for a man to take the first step and it would never happen. But if the man does call, she believes that he is interested in her and that sex has nothing to do with it. So, who picks who in a relationship? On the other hand, if she decides to go home from the club with him for sex, she would end up giving him her phone number, he would say that he would give her a call, but that call will never come. In the end, she'll feel bad for having sex with that person, she'll feel used for getting involved in a one night stand and she'll also feel guilty and less of a woman.

Don't cheat yourself, do not let him or her manipulate the situation, do not be in a hurry; be patient.

Trying too hard to have a relationship

Sometimes either the man or woman tries too hard to secure a relationship, between the two, none should do this. Things like tracking them down to find out where they live, rushing to have sex, calling constantly, and spending so much on them are bad ideas. In the beginning, it is not good to do whatever he/she asks in that relationship; there should be clearly stated boundaries. There are tests to see how far they can go and how far you are willing to let them go. If they have control over the relationship, they will take advantage of you. Do not try too hard to get anyone to be with you; nobody should try too hard to be with anybody. What does that tell you about that relationship? You are going into that relationship with the wrong attitude and mindset. Never let a person see how much you care in the beginning. I believe you should show kindness and love for someone with potentials, but do not rush into anything; study the person first. So, who picks who in the relationship?

It was all about the sex and sex is not always love

A relationship that is founded on sex started with sex. The two-people probably met each other in a club, but it led to sex. If he is spending more time on sex than on dates with you, then he's getting exactly what he wants; sex. If that's all he ever wants to do with you, that is all you will get from him. If you continue to meet, nothing will change, because the relationship was founded on the wrong thing -Sex. When one of the individuals starts to develop feelings for the other and tells the other, he/she will ask why the other wants to mess up a good thing. They always refuse to talk about a real relationship, or about taking the relationship to the next level because they've gotten or are getting what they want. He/she does not see the other person as anything more than a sex object. This is especially the case when it comes to women. Women should not be so hasty to have sex because in the end, they lose out. Men and women feel different, and women at the more emotional between the two. Women should have more respect for themselves; they should not get manipulated by men. If your relationship begins with sex, it probably may never turn out the way you would like it to. Woman, please do not let him talk you into having sex. No one can talk you into doing anything that you do not like or want to do. If you get convinced, then you wanted it just as much as the other person. You got exactly what you wanted. So decide, is it all for sex? Remember you can't have a real relationship with that mindset. So, who picks who in the relationship?

Was not looking for a relationship but it happened?

I know fully of the "I'm not looking for a relationship right now" category. Please don't be alarmed when they tell you they are not looking for anything serious. Every man and every woman may not want to have a relationship, but if it happens, it happens. You see, when this man saw the woman, she was just another beautiful person. He then tells her, "We must go out sometime." He knows nothing about her, but when they meet up, she lets him know that she was not looking for a man because she just got out of a relationship. But then this man and woman started spending time together and sex was not a factor. A relationship is formed between them, and it grows. Because they've spent quality time together, they become friends and understand one another. To make it even better, the relationship is based on their prayers for each other. No one is dominant in this relationship and they respect each other.

Once you pick the person you want to be with and you start spending quality time together, going to the movie, cycling, just going for some walks, sitting around and talking, playing games, you talk on the phone, have weekend getaways and spend time with each other's families; the relationship will continue to grow with every passing day.

CHAPTER 2

IT IS A NEW DAY

You've been dating for a year, two or even three and you keep fending off people that ask "when are you two going to get married," you think that you've found "The One" But have you? After so many years together, you assume he must be the one. That's what I thought. He leads you on and says things like I'm going to marry you, he even proposes but never gives you a ring. It is wrong to think, as we all do, that women just need the validation of the proposal more than an actual wedding. Do you really believe that women just want validation of the proposal more than an actual wedding? Think again! You are kidding yourself if you think that all women want are marriage proposals. Men need to set a date and go through with the wedding. If a man has not set a date yet, stop letting him make excuses. How long are you going to hold on to a proposal for a marriage that might not take place? I believe that a woman should not be engaged for up to two or three years before marriage. If he tells you things like I would like to get my finances together, I need to plan for retirement, etcetera, you need to recognize that these are signs that he is just playing with your feelings. I do not believe he will get married to you; this is because he is afraid of a commitment and just wants to control and mess with your mind. Unfortunately, one thing about some women is that they want to get married so bad that they will sit there and let him take advantage of the situation. If a man is 65 years old, he can get a woman of 25 or a 50-year old to get involved with, and even end up marrying her. But if a woman is from 55 to 60 years old, she might never get married because of her age. It would be difficult for her to get a 25 or 50-year-old man to marry her. Remember they're books out there on marriage that can help you make the right decision, books that guide you in relationships, just like this book. Please pay attention to lessons from such books. Make use of what you have heard or read to discover what's going on in your life; if you're in a dead-end relationship, if you're setting the right example or if you have a daughter or son that needs some advice. If you have a son, he should not take advantage of women, and if you have a daughter teach her to be careful so that she would not be taken advantage of.

For the woman that is in a manipulative relationship, there are signs. The hard part is not just seeing them but going through them. Give thanks, get out and live your life without relying on a proposal to make you happy. Life isn't a joke, but if you have some doubts, these are indicators that he's not in a place to marry you. He does not want to marry you, and you'll thank him years from now for not doing it.

1. About the Future

It is generally not a promising idea to discuss marriage and babies on the first date, because it can be a very uncomfortable conversation. However, at some point in the relationship, it is a requirement. But if you and your guy talk about jobs, careers, rent, trips, family and holidays, you should trust the relationship enough to discuss your future. Otherwise, it becomes an unpleasant conversation whenever it is brought up. That awkwardness is one of the signs that you are involved with the wrong person; this just causes more doubt and uneasiness. You'll be surprised how this type of discussion isn't so scary or difficult with the right guy.

2. Be Successful, Financially Secure

There is intense pressure for men to be the breadwinners in a family. Even though most women I know are successful, it's understandable that most men want to know they can provide for their wife and family. While there is a time and place to focus on a career or education, to constantly hear "I'm not in a place to marry anyone right now" is confusing and frustrating. It keeps a relationship in limbo. Also, it repeatedly tells the woman that this decision isn't hers. Instead, it is when he is "ready." Who knows the tough times couples may face together in the future?

Before you get married, share your financial story with your significant other, you need to know exactly where you stand. Your assessment should include valuable information about your current financial status. Review your income and your recent expenses. Then, create a spending plan so you can keep track of income and expenses.

Create a debt reduction plan. You don't have to eliminate your credit cards or student loan or debt to walk down the aisle. But it is important to at least have an action plan in place to do so as quickly as possible after exchanging your "wedding vows." Many couples delay getting married because of debt. Take the following steps:

1. Get your credit reports
2. Learn your partner's financial past and present.
3. Decide on joint or separate accounts.
4. Outline income and spending patterns.
5. Set goals and track your progress
6. Know your partner's spending habits
7. **Schedule monthly budget talks dealing with money.**
8. Plan a wedding you can afford
9. Decide who pays the bills
10. How will you handle money in your household?
11. Discuss financial goals.
12. Discuss how much is going out/coming in.
13. Figure out how much money needs to be in your emergency savings.
14. Create a budget.
15. Establish a five-year plan and ten-year plan.
16. Make sure you have the right insurance.

Please, before getting married, perform everything on this checklist.

3. Doesn't Know

A couple moved in together and started looking at rings; she thought he was The One. However, months later, she asked, "Do you still want to marry me?" she was shocked when he responded, "I don't know." Living together, he still "didn't know," but deep down inside he knew. If you feel confident that you are with the man you want to marry, you can tell when things have changed, and what is really going on at every point in the relationship. No one should take marriage lightly; at some point, you must lay all your cards on the table. What other information does he think he needs to know before tying the knot? When in doubt, ask a direct question? It may not be what you want to hear, but it's the truth. It is obvious in this scenario that they're in an unbalanced relationship; unequally yoked, and I believe she should move out and get her own place, yes. The breakup would probably be rough but eventually, your soul mate or your husband will come along.

4. Her Problem is

It is not that you're attracting the wrong men? The truth is that you always accept the wrong man. When you have been dating a man for two (or three) years and he hasn't proposed, the problem is that you have accepted the way the relationship is. When you are dating a man who is verbally and physically abusive, who says he loves you but shuts down when you attempt to have a discussion with him about the future, it is because you have accepted him that way.

I'm not encouraging you not to accept the flaws of men. I'm telling you that if you think you are attracting flawed men, you're incorrect, you're only accepting them.

5. His Problem is

It is not that you are attracting the wrong women. The truth is that you always accept the wrong woman. When you have been dating a woman for two (or three) years, and she is not ready to make any commitment, it is because you have accepted her way she is. When you are dating a woman who is verbally and physically abusive, who, although you love her, always shuts you down when you attempt to discuss settling down, it occurs because you have accepted her.

I'm not encouraging you not to accept the flaws of a woman. I'm telling you that if you think you are attracting flawed women, you're incorrect, you're only accepting them.

2 Corinthians 6:14-16(KJV)

Be ye not unequally yoked together with unbelievers: for what fellowship hath righteousness with unrighteousness? and what communion hath light with darkness?

WHEN YOU DON'T REALIZE THAT YOU ARE IN A GOOD RELATIONSHIP

Some women do not realize when they have a good man

A woman once asked me, why does it seem like men always choose to be serious with other women, when he says he doesn't want to commit to the girl he's dating. What I would like you women to do is, close your eyes for a few minutes and think about how you really treat your guy. Yes, you can say he was the problem but remember it is not all about him. It is also about you, so take this test truthfully. If you do not, you will never understand why he did not choose you; you will continue doing the same thing in every relationship until you truly understand, take responsibility and accept that deep down inside you knew what the problem was.

Even though I believe men are simple, every man has his reasons for leaving a woman. For the record, regardless of what they say, I think men are always looking for a serious, committed relationship. Maybe he's just not that into her; maybe he was too into you; maybe he was once into her, but then he stopped being into you.

I can't speak on the specific reason why a man leaves a woman, but I can speak on why it seems like men eventually settle down with another woman they get involved with after claiming they didn't want a commitment. You can't say without a doubt that your ex got with the other woman he dated. Maybe he dated several women before meeting the right woman. However, I guess that's not very comforting to hear. For the sake of it, let's assume your ex made a serious commitment to the other woman he dated after you.

How could this happen, after he told you several times, in so many words and actions, that a serious commitment wasn't what he was looking for? What he said at that point may have been true, because he probably did not see the possibility of a committed relationship or marriage with you in the future. Maybe he was still looking for that right person. He may have met someone special and saw something in that person; it could have been the way she smiled or the way she carried herself or just maybe the words that came from her mouth when he struck up a conversation. This is why it's very important for you to do a self-examination! Make sure that before your next relationship, the problem that drove your ex away is fixed.

Let me share this thought with you; not every woman spends hours fantasizing about getting married, and not every man goes to the altar jumping up and down in excitement. But there are lots of women in bad relationships who think the only problem is that he hasn't proposed. These women are ready to waste years with a guy who is never going to marry them. In my opinion, males are born, but men are made. Every relationship, good or bad, is a learning experience for men. I'm sure this applies to women, too. However, when it comes to relationships, most men learn how to become men through trial and error. As a man, it's easy to learn how to operate independently, but a man must be in a relationship or several to learn what's expected of him as a man in a relationship. Stated differently, being a good man doesn't automatically make a man good in a relationship. Every failed relationship is a learning opportunity. Whether we like it or not, many of us have helped or been a part of someone's life as they improved as a person. They took those new skills to benefit their next relationship. This truth makes some women feel like they were used to make him a good man. They also feel like the qualities needed to succeed in the next relationship were gained from them, but despite their years of loyalty and sacrifice, when the time came for the man to commit, he chose to take the new skills to someone else. They apply all they learned from the first relationship in their next relationship, and as a result, don't make all the same mistakes with the new woman. After all, you only learn how not to make the same mistakes twice. The same can be said for a relationship. It teaches men how to be better men. The woman's sacrifice of time and effort are rewarded with a commitment, but there is no guarantee, especially if there was never a commitment to begin with. Honestly, most men know when they want to be with a woman and when they don't want to. In actuality, he needs to be better prepared, older and mature when the opportunity for a committed relationship presents itself.

Some men do not realize when they have a good woman

I'm sure now that no matter how good a woman is to a man, he's not ready to be with her. You could cook every meal for him, wash his clothes, and buy him everything that he wanted and please him around the clock, cater for him, love him, and give him everything he asks for; but if he's not ready for a commitment, he won't make one.

I'm just going to keep it real; these men know they have a good woman, but they just want to take advantage of them. They make these women feel less of who they are, thereby controlling them; it's not right. If you do not want to be with her, please let her go. Do not waste her time while robbing her of her happiness. I'm disappointed in men who do this because the Bible says in Proverbs 18:22 He who finds a wife finds a good thing and obtains favor from the Lord. Yes, I know that the Bible says if you find a wife you have a good thing, but when a woman believes she has a good man, she will do what she can to show her appreciation. When he is down, she is there for him. When he is sick, she caters for his health. She has his back if anyone comes against him. She will suffer through hard times with him believing he will do the same for her. When he is out among his friends and others, he refers to her as just a friend, but when he comes to her home, she becomes his lady. She is his lady only in her home. What's a man's motive for doing this? He tells the women in secret that she is his woman but tells his friends she is just a friend. Some men only do this to be in a safe place while they prey on other women, not realizing they are hurting the good women in their lives. A man that does this doesn't realize that all that he is doing to fulfill his selfish needs will eventually come back to hurt him. When he needs help, he may not get it. He may look back and see that all the women he hurt have moved on, but he is alone. He may end up sick or broke; either way, he ends up down and out. He may never know what's heading his way when he hurts so many people. The best thing to do is to tell the truth about what you want in a relationship, and let that person decide if that is the kind of relationship they want to remain in. There is too much hurt in this world and many people cannot recover from this type of hurt. Just remember, hurting people hurt others, and you don't want to create a person that will cause hurt to another person. There is a thin line between "Love and Pain."

As a woman, you can't change a man; this is because all you do is what your heart feels. All you can do is give yourself to someone and love them without limits, and if you get that back that's great, but if not, move on to someone who can love you the way you deserve to be loved. Trust and believe that there is someone out there that can love you and put their heart in a relationship the same way you do.

To the men that keep hurting good woman, a time will come when she will put her foot down and say she deserves better. You will be shocked! Most men think that day will never come. And that point, they realize that they just lost the best thing that ever came into their life. Don't let the blessing that has been bestowed upon you get away.

People say a relationship is 50%/50%. I don't believe that a relationship should be based on each person's 100%. If you put 50% in and he/she put 50% too, where are you putting the other 50% of your commitment to that relationship? Are you investing it in another person? If you want a relationship to work. Don't say 50/50, put your 100% into that relationship.

Here is a list of disrespectful behaviors that no woman should ever tolerate.

1. Arriving late at home or on a date with no excuse.
2. Not even showing up at all.
3. Constantly canceling dates and rescheduling.
4. Lying about his whereabouts.
5. Lying about seeing other women (or sleeping with other women).
6. Remarks about how you look after which he puts you down and tease you about your weight
7. Flirting with or making sexual comments about other women.
8. Making promises he doesn't keep.
9. Introducing you as a friend, when you are his girlfriend.

THEN YOU START TO DATE

Once you pick the person you want to be with, start spending quality time together. Like going to the movie, going cycling, going for a walk or just sitting around and playing games and spending time with each other. When you do this, the relationship will grow continually. You will become really interested in that person and the feeling will be mutual. This is only the beginning of the relationship, you have a long way to go. How you proceed in this early stage of the relationship in the next few days, weeks or months will determine whether it will become a real and lasting relationship. Do not discuss your relationship status and updates with all your friends, because everyone does not want your happiness. Keeping things private is important, so you can avoid embarrassment in case things don't work out. He or She should just hold back on showing signs of desperation for a relationship. At least be in the relationship for four to six months, before you declare he/she to be 'the one.'

Give each other space for the relationship to grow

Always remember that it is important to give space; it can be tempting to be in touch with your new girlfriend or boyfriend all day and all night. Technology has made it easier to maintain this level of communication; you can either text, email or make phone calls. However, too much contact can easily hurt a new relationship. There needs to be time and space for you to miss each other so that you can be expectant of the next call or date. If calls and texts are coming every thirty minutes, what is there to look forward to? Avoid showing desperation; there is no need for you to contact each other within every thirty minutes.

Getting on each other nerves

Don't be surprised and do not fool yourself in any relationship, you both will get on each other's nerves; yes, you're dating, yes, you're in love, but she would say things that will get on your nerves and he will say things to get on your nerves too. At the end of the day if two people love each other they should be able to resolve their differences.

Never reveal too much too soon about yourself

We all have a past and have had previous relationships. You should never go into a new relationship telling them your life story so soon. There will be a time when you will share a part of your deep secrets and past relationships. You will surely share these with each other, but pouring all your emotional baggage too soon will likely hurt any chance of a future together. I am not advising you to keep secrets, but wait for the right time to discuss your past. If you want the relationship to last a lifetime, then you must be willing to spend a lifetime getting to know each other. The first few weeks and months are the time to have fun, get to know each other, find out what makes each other tick, and look forward to seeing each other. Also, explore what you enjoy doing together.

Show that you appreciate that person

There is no better way to show how you are feeling than being appreciative. Being appreciative can help secure a long-lasting relationship between you both. Right from the beginning, even when on dates, always show your appreciation by saying things like "thank you for your compliments" or "it has been lovely talking to you," "I enjoy being with you." If one person chooses somewhere good for a date, the other person should appreciate the choice. If they have a nice attitude and personality, tell them things like, "I enjoy your company."

Furthermore, always remember to say something nice to Him are Her about their clothes, their hair, their eyes or even the way they smell. If something they did or said made you feel happy, let them know. These are just random examples; what is important is that you get into the practice of saying nice appreciative things, you just may have made their day by doing that.

Do not forget that you had a life

One of the biggest mistakes couples make at the beginning of a relationship is putting aside the things they were doing before they met. They put their life on hold and devote all their time and attention to their new relationship. They forget that they went out with friends; had hobbies and interests; went to work and generally had a full life. Once your partner gets to know you and see all that you've cast aside or neglected, not only will that say something about your loyalty and commitment, but it can place too much pressure on as your all and everything.

Make sure he/she is the right one; there is no rush

Enjoy every moment of your new relationship, and remember there is no rush to move on to the next stage. Be understanding of the other person's feelings; don't try to rush them in the relationship before they are ready. Like talking on the phone meeting their friends; letting them know where you live; introducing them to your family or showing them to your children if you have. If you try and do it all too soon, you may scare them off. Do not let sex, being too pushy or too anxious be a factor in their decision making.

CHAPTER 3

WHEN DID THEY KNOW THEY FELL IN LOVE?

2 Corinthians 6:14-16(KJV)

Be ye not unequally yoked together with unbelievers: for what fellowship hath righteousness with unrighteousness? And what communion hath light with darkness?

Yes, it would be great if the two people who meet are equally yoked. But we know realistically that people who are dating and getting married are not equally yoked; they get involved and get married for the wrong reason. So is love in every situation? No, but it should. This is why couples should be equally yoked based on God's word.

I believe without a doubt that a person would know if He or she has fallen in love after being in a relationship for about six months. When something like the loss of a loved one happens in either of their family; He or She comforts the other. He or she also helps when the other is going through financial difficulties. If He or She gets massively sick, the partner will take care of him or her without any hesitation whatsoever. When you see your girlfriend or boyfriend picking up your nasty tissues and helping you to find a way to get your finances in order, even if it wasn't an issue he or she knew, He or she should be the one you should marry. Obviously, you enjoy being with that person, and the person just genuinely wants to make you feel better. That moment when you realize what you have is a pretty special moment.

When we got into our first huge fight, I was expecting she would tell me to leave or to sleep on the couch, but she just said, 'What are you doing? We need to talk about this now because if we are going to have a committed relationship, we need to learn how to sit down and discuss how to fix our problems throughout this relationship."

You will always have some disagreements or arguments with your partner. But the most important thing is how you solve any problem you encounter in that relationship. First, both of you need to apologize, ask for forgiveness, kiss and makeup. Try not to let such things happen again in the relationship.

She likes to watch football games with me and I like going to the mall with her. They both love to work on projects together. "This is the woman I'm going to marry" were just thoughts till she said, "this is the man she going to marry."

"When I brought her home to meet my family, I observed how she interacted with everyone. My mother was in the kitchen cooking and she just volunteered to help in the kitchen. She helped in cooking, washed the dishes while laughing and having fun being real. I saw how well she could fit with the people I loved, and it was game over for me. I was even more convinced that She was the one."

"When I brought him home to meet my family, I observed how he interacted with everyone. My father was watching the football game and he joined him, "I like him" my father said. My mother also liked him, they were laughing, having fun and he was just real. I saw how well he could fit with the people I loved, and it was game over for me. He was/ is the one."

We've never actually said I love you, we use the word I like you a whole lot.' But the first time we used the sentence I love you on each other, we realized that we were really in love with each other.

GETTING ENGAGED

When you are seriously dating someone, and you are thinking about marrying that person, committing yourself to that person is a huge decision. If you choose the wrong person, you could suffer years of heartache, or wind up in an abusive marriage or even a divorce. However, if you choose wisely, you could enjoy a lifetime of intimate love and passion. No marriage is easy or perfect.

Some couple's rush towards marriage as soon as they taste the thrill of romance. They may have only dated for a few months, but the thrill of romance convinces them that they are destined for each other. Another couple dates for many years but never find the courage to make a commitment, because they fear that they may marry the wrong person. For this reason, they do not get married at all. Can a single person make the right decision?

The good news is that if you are a born-again Christian, you are not alone in your decision-making process. You have Jesus Christ within you. He offers you His wisdom in every situation so that you don't have to rely upon your own emotions and wisdom. Also, God has given us his wisdom, so that we can know the wonderful things that He has freely given us, but the people who aren't Christians can't understand the true wisdom that comes from God. How could they?

Genesis 2:24 states, "For this reason a man shall leave his father and his mother, and be joined to his wife; and they shall become one flesh.

1 Corinthians 2:12(KJV)

12 Now we have received, not the spirit of the world, but the spirit which is of God; that we might know the things that are freely given to us of God.

1 Corinthians 2:14(KJV)

14 But the natural man receiveth not the things of the Spirit of God: for they are foolishness unto him: neither can he know them, because they are spiritually discerned.

1 Corinthians 2:16(KJV)

16 for who hath known the mind of the Lord, that he may instruct him? but we have the mind of Christ.

2 Corinthians 6:14(KJV)

14 Be ye not unequally yoked together with unbelievers: for what fellowship hath righteousness with unrighteousness? And what communion hath light with darkness?

2 Corinthians 6:15(KJV)

15 And what concord hath Christ with Belial? or what part hath he that believeth with an infidel?

2 Corinthians 6:16(KJV)

16 And what agreement hath the temple of God with idols? for ye are the temple of the living God; as God hath said, I will dwell in them, and walk in them; and I will be their God, and they shall be my people.

God wants the best for you. He gave you the mind of Christ so that you can see life from His perspective. Jesus can work through your heart and mind to direct you toward a good relationship and dissuade you from a bad one. However, you can only discern His counsel when you are willing to listen and yield to Him.

Romantic passion is the wrong foundation for a marriage. Jesus wants you to give your heart to someone because of character and passionate sacrificial love. To help you assess if your relationship contains these elements, consider taking the self-examination below before you get engaged.

Are You Both Born Again?

This question is the most important question to be answered in a relationship and it is spiritual. If you or your fiancé do not know Jesus as the main source of love, you will try to manipulate love from one another, depending on your relationship with each other. Love is like taking a walk on the beach, it may feel good for a moment, but it cannot satisfy you. Your heart needs more than romance; it needs affection and understanding to survive. It needs unconditional love, which can only be found in Jesus Christ. Thus, it is best to marry someone who understands that he or she is married to Jesus first, and realizes the importance of depending on Him for fulfillment.

Yes, it can be difficult to find this kind of person, however, if you believe that you can enjoy intimacy with a non-Christian date then, don't marry them. Many Christians make this mistake and it cheats them out of the inheritance of a Christian marriage. They rely on human nature and are ready to get married to the first person that comes along. As Christians, we are united in Jesus Christ. This means that the same Jesus who lives within him should also live within her. Therefore, He can help them both love one another more deeply.

Are you at risk when you are dating or marrying a non-Christian? If you join yourself to an unbeliever, you will be incapable of sharing real intimacy. You are free to date a non-Christian person but the Bible states that it is not profitable. God views believers and unbelievers as opposites who have no potential for a deep union.

2 Corinthians 6:14(KJV)

14 Be ye not unequally yoked together with unbelievers: for what fellowship hath righteousness with unrighteousness? And what communion hath light with darkness?

1 Corinthians 7:39(KJV)

39 The wife is bound by the law as long as her husband liveth; but if her

husband be dead, she is at liberty to be married to whom she will; only in the Lord.

Can a Christian get along with an unbeliever and have fun dating him or her? Sure. In fact, some non-Christians relationship exhibits just as much honesty and sensitivity as some Christians do. However, if you marry an unbeliever, he or she will generally have a larger influence on the direction of your relationship. The non-Christian can influence the relationship by having the Christian do things of the world that they would not normally do.

1. A Christian cannot overpower a non-Christian's free will and force him or her to accept Christ.
2. An unbeliever might mislead you, just to gain your acceptance.

If you try to convert someone to Christ just so you can date or marry him or her, you could cloud that person's spiritual decision with human romance. In addition, if someone professes faith in Christ solely so that he or she can date you, the person is probably not a Christian. A person becomes a Christian when he or she genuinely asks for forgiveness of sin and accepts Christ as Lord of his or her life. Even if you lead someone to accept Christ, he or she may need years to develop the maturity necessary for sacrificial love in marriage.

Can You Resolve Conflict Together?

You date, get married, and then conflict hits. They are unaware that two imperfect people experience friction no matter how much they love each other. Conflict is an unavoidable part of life, and it can and will destroy a couple who haven't learned how to resolve it properly.

Conflict can influence you in ways contrary to the desires that Christ puts within you. You might feel tempted to be insensitive, greedy, self-indulgent, manipulative, or hostile. When you yield to these temptations in a relationship, a simple disagreement can escalate into a major argument.

Only through your faith can Christ help you resolve your issues. As a couple, you both must yield to His desires. So, it is important that you deal with conflict several times before considering engagement. Determine whether both of you have shown a desire to compromise in past arguments. If not, does one of you try to intimidate the other with anger or by being loud? If you've had trouble handling disagreements, consider dating longer to learn how to disagree and reconcile and if nothing improves, you may need to end your relationship. Arguments can benefit a relationship by exposing neglect, unrealistic expectations, or different points of view. Sometimes, neither person is wrong. But each person approaches the same topic with different perspectives.

Therefore, do not try to avoid conflict; however, seek to resolve it in a loving and understanding manner. If you cannot freely voice your opinions, you will live in miserable bondage to another person. Both partners should have the freedom to express their ideas and desires openly in the relationship.

A relationship that is devoid of conflict signals that one of you is either too passive or too afraid to be genuine. These attitudes are not conducive to have an intimate marriage, and you should not continue dating if you cannot be real with each other. A healthy relationship establishes an environment in which you have the freedom to disagree. Thus, before you get engaged, make sure you both feel free to be yourselves, also make sure you both know how to resolve conflict lovingly.

How You Both Dealt with Your Baggage?

Weather dating or getting married, the two is striving to become one. By the time we reach adulthood, we are all inevitably carrying some sort of baggage with us. Baggage can surface in many forms, such as addictions, eating disorders, abortion, debt, abusive relationship or divorce. Unfortunately, everyone carries some type of baggage, so do not assume that your boyfriend or girlfriend is immune from baggage. Before you give someone your heart, determine if he or she has a lot of baggage and issues that you can deal with. There is no perfect person; we all hold our own baggage. If you are interested in someone, a time will come when you'll make a choice to invest time in that person. The question is, "will their baggage be a deal breaker?" When you make a choice to seek out the person of your choice, you might want to remember that the two of you are two different individuals coming together, this means that there will be differences. To teach each other, you both need to know that every disagreement is neither an argument nor a battle. Learn to pick your battles; small disagreements are just another person's point of view. Learn to respect each other's opinion; it does not mean they are always right; it just the way they view it. Remember you are learning this individual, and if there are too many views you don't' agree with...**IT'S-A DEAL BREAKER;** this person is not who you want. Too many times, couples just settle, thinking things will change when they get married; many times, that doesn't work out. The end result for this type of assumption is divorce because they can't live with the ways of their spouse. Learn to identify the baggage you don't want but have the understanding that you will have to pick some baggage. Understand that certain baggage may never disappear completely.

An addiction can keep someone in poor health. A divorced single may regularly have child custody problems. If you want to marry someone who happens to have these kinds of issues, you might face very tough circumstances when the person's past resurfaces. If you are not prepared to deal with them, the repercussions could easily dominate your relationship. Discuss your concerns with your Pastor or a Christian counselor if you feel unsure about how someone's past might affect you. Please do not downplay it because every baggage is real, and it has the power to destroy your relationship. Sometimes, these complex, negative issues require years to resolve. Do not expect that marriage will make them disappear. You will have to wait until a person overcomes his or her baggage with the truth of God's love before real healing takes place. Therefore, if your boyfriend or girlfriend carries emotional baggage, please deal with it before you get engaged. Marrying someone who is free of baggage is worth the extra months or years of waiting.

Do not misunderstand me. I am not saying that you should not marry a person with baggage, I am saying, make sure you are able to deal with the baggage that comes with the person. Do not regret it later; be careful. If you do not solve the problems, you will be walking down the aisle with a problem you will spend the rest of your life with. If you are seeking a relationship with someone younger than you, have in mind that as the older adult, you have more life experience and may be more set in your ways. Becoming one with a much younger person can be difficult, as your ways of thinking can be worlds apart. But look at the bright side you could bring wisdom with you along with some wonderful experience.

Do You Have the Support of Friends and Family?

After Genise and I had dated for ten months, many of our close friends and relatives started asking when we were going to get married or if the question had been popped yet, when I asked why, they said, "We think she is a great girl," and "We think you guys are a good fit for each other." I took those comments to heart. They were sincere because she and I had spent a lot of time around our friends and family. Their opinion meant something because they had been a part of our relationship. Since I knew they wanted the best for us, their opinion reinforced my desire to marry her.

In the same way, I encourage you to seek support from your friends and family, since these people know you. However, always have in mind that there is the need to have at least two people you can trust and confide in. Everyone does not want to see you happy. Also, everyone is not as emotionally blind as you are, and as a result, some close friends may identify problem areas that you have overlooked.

Should someone raise a concern about your relationship, focus on the facts, do not hide the truth. Be willing to admit that you might have a problem. You should consider that they may have many years of marriage experience to back up their concerns, and ignoring them would be foolish. Listen with an open mind to what they say about your relationship. Remember, however, that the final decision is no one's but yours to make. It lies solely in your hands. Parents and friends are allowed to express their feelings but don't allow them to decide for you. When you make one of the biggest decisions of your life, having the support of your family and friends is a wonderful blessing. It does not only gives you a sense of peace; it also assures you that they will be there for you if times get hard. No married couple is a rock.

Leadership role in Your Relationship

You must understand that Christ is the head of every man, and the man is the head of a woman. God is the head of Christ for man did not come from a woman, but a woman came from a man; for indeed man was not created for the woman's sake, but a woman was created for the sake of man.

Ephesians 5:23-25(KJV)

23 For the husband is the head of the wife, even as Christ is the head of the church: and he is the saviour of the body.

24 Therefore as the church is subject unto Christ, so let the wives be to their own husbands in everything.

25 Husbands, love your wives, even as Christ also loved the church, and gave himself for it;

This scripture clearly explains how God established the leadership role of husbands and wives in marriage. Consider the following points:

1. God is the Head of Christ.
2. Jesus is the Head of every man and woman.
3. A husband is the head of his wife.
4. A woman is subject to her husband.
5. A husband is to love his wife sacrificially, just as Christ loves the church.
6. Men and women are not independent of each other.

Remember, God is the one that established the leadership roles, and he designated Christ and men as the leaders. However, they choose whether to assume that responsibility. Obviously, Jesus always obeys His Father and respects His leadership.

John 5:30(KJV)

30 I can of mine own self do nothing: as I hear, I judge: and my judgment is just; because I seek not mine own will, but the will of the Father which hath sent me.

A husband faces the choice of whether to follow Christ's leadership. When a husband tries to lead his wife independently of Christ's leadership, he sins. Likewise, God calls a wife to follow her husband.

Examine Your Passion

After examining your relationship with these questions; you may not feel at peace about committing to your boyfriend or girlfriend anymore. That's okay. The advantage of dating is so that you can learn who someone is before giving them your heart. Your discomfort may be the Lord urging you to date longer or to separate. If you break up, be glad that you avoided an unwise marriage decision.

As husband and wife, we are still amazed by how our hearts continue to unite in many ways. Our marriage has surpassed our wildest dreams of what romance, friendship, and love could ever be. We owe this pleasure to Christ, who pursued us with such love so much so that we want to share it with others. Likewise, if Jesus is inspiring you to give yourself to someone special, take the time to pour His love into that person and pour out his passion into the relationship that He has set up for the both of you to explore, amen.

WHEN YOU GET MARRIED

A person can say, "I never thought that I would have to get married." When my husband proposed to me, there were plenty of things to consider before I agreed to marry him. I considered his eyes and realized that for the first time, I was at least willing to try because it was a big step for me.

Marriage can only be between a man and a woman.

God defined marriage in Genesis 2:24 states, "For this reason a man shall leave his father and his mother, and be joined to his wife; and they shall become one flesh." Marriage can only be between a man and a woman, and they are joined together as a single entity. It involves leaving old things, a life of childhood and starting something new.

There are many kinds of unions between people. However, that does not mean its marriage. Living together may be a type of union, but it does not mean that you are married. And, to answer the question of the so-called "homosexual marriage." By biblical definition, marriage can only be between a man and a woman, so homosexual unions are not recognized as marriages by the constitution of Heaven. It cannot be; yes, the Supreme Court can change the law and say that a union between the same sex is marriage, you can even get a marriage license but in the eyes of God, it is not right. If the union between two men or two women is right, why should, or would homosexuals try to make everyone accept them? When a man and a woman get married, they do not try to make you accept their union because it is natural. You may use some other term to describe homosexual relationships, but to use the word marriage is incorrect. The biblical definition does not allow it.

Marriage is more than a commitment.

A couple can say they have made their vows to each other and consummated the relationship; they can further state that nowhere in the bible does it state you have to go through a 'ceremony' to get married, and they feel that what they did was enough. They felt that making vows to each other was enough to constitute a marriage in the eyes of God. However, the Bible does take a different view.

You see, marriage is more than just committing to someone. It is also entering a holy covenant before God. In Malachi, God rebukes the people of Judah for not following His laws. There we read, the Lord has been a witness between you and the wife of your youth, against whom you have dealt treacherously, though she is your companion and your wife by covenant... For I hate divorce,' says the Lord." (Mal 2:14, 16). (For more on divorce, please see "In Matthew 19: 3-9 KJV).

God says here that marriage is a covenant, one witnessed and sealed by Him. A commitment is a civil agreement. A covenant is religious by nature and should be presided over by a religious official. Breaking a commitment can be done by agreement. However, a covenant is considered binding and can only be broken if God has provided a dissolution, such as in the case of adultery.

Marriage is to be witnessed.

Because marriage is a covenant to be entered freely by two individuals; a man and a woman, it must be witnessed by at least two or three people. This idea is confirmed in Matthew 18:16, where Jesus quotes Leviticus, "Out of the mouth of two or three witnesses every fact may be confirmed."

Ruth 4:9-12 shows this applies specifically to marriage when Boaz seeks out witnesses to secure his right to marry Ruth, the Moabitess. There, the witnesses even pronounce a marriage blessing on them.

Marriage is to be held in honor.

If we take all of the above into account, we can see that marriage is an institution not to be taken lightly. In fact, a union of marriage is an honor. "Marriage is to be held in honor among all, and the marriage bed is to be undefiled..." (Heb. 13:4KJV)

4 Marriage is honourable in all, and the bed undefiled: but whoremongers and adulterers God will judge.

We know that marriage is honorable, and the Bible commands us to render its honor properly. Further, it shows that we are to obey the governing laws and respect the customs associated with Biblical marriage. Our laws recognize that the holy union of marriage is entered by a man and a woman. It also recognizes the covenant nature of marriage; this is why a clergy is required to perform marriage ceremonies and why witnesses are required. Therefore, to give marriage proper honor and to render the proper respect to the authorities, legal marriage is both required and appropriate. Taking all this into account, the Bible clearly shows that an official marriage ceremony performed by a clergy is a good way of entering marriage appropriately.

Protestant Wedding Vows

There are several types of vows, all with their own slightly different traditions and beliefs. Below are basic wedding vows from various denominations. Though the vows are from different denominations, you'll find that many of them differ only slightly from one another.

Basic Protestant Vows

"I, ___, take thee, ___, to be my wedded husband/wife, to have and to hold, from this day forward, for better, for worse, for richer, for poorer, in sickness and in health, to love and to cherish, till death do us part, according to God's holy ordinance; and thereto I pledge thee my faith [or] pledge myself to you."

Catholic Wedding Vows

"I, ___, take you, ___, for my lawful wife/husband, to have and to hold from this day forward, for better, for worse, for richer, for poorer, in sickness and health, until death do us part."

"I, ___, take you, ___, to be my husband/wife. I promise to be true to you in good times and in bad, in sickness and in health. I will love and honor you all the days of my life."

Personalizing your wedding vows is a wonderful way to reflect upon your relationship.

In today's weddings, couples do not understand the vows they make between one another. Even though God Almighty is in the company of witnesses, they take these vows as a joke; they do not respect them, nor do they take them seriously. If they really listen to those vows, they will have a better understanding and respect the covenant they made between one another.

CHAPTER 4

ALL ISSUES THAT COME WITH MARRIAGE

If you ever talk to married couples, one thing you are bound to hear is that marriage is hard. Once that honeymoon period ends and the two of you are back to real life, it takes a lot of time and effort to make the marriage work. There are plenty of problems that will inevitably come up but, thankfully, most of them can be solved quite easily. Here are some of the marriage problems that you may face after tying the knot:

Financial Struggle

No matter how little or how much you make, at some point, the money will come up as an issue during your marriage. It can be hard to talk about money problems objectively, and you may notice that the two of you become defensive and testy in no time. Sadly, money issues are often tied to emotional ones.

I believe that one of the major themes of the Bible is obedience to the Lord. These financial principles are real, and obedience to them demonstrates that the Christian is trusting God in other areas of their lives.

God is the Source

God is the source of everything. Philippians 4:19(KJV)

"My God shall supply all your need according to his riches in glory by Christ Jesus."

He or She is Messy; you're not

When he or she comes home, they both do things like, taking shoes off at the door and tossing stockings under the family room table. The lady might take off her stockings and put them on the floor in the bedroom or leave chips open on the kitchen table. Believe it or not, this problem is common; lack of cleanliness can easily become a significant issue in a marriage.

You're the household maid

When the house needs to be thoroughly cleaned, you find out that your husband is out or completely uninterested in the task at hand. Not only does he make some of the mess, he never has much interest in cleaning it up. This means that you're left with the brunt of the work. Having to clean an entire house on your own can be tiring, annoying, and frustrating.

The marriage now includes his mom or her mom

Before getting married, it can be hard to determine whether his or her mom will be an ideal mother-in-law or not. While some will readily leave you to your marriage, some moms will want to stick their noses in everything. The signs are usually already there if you're marrying a mama's boy or mama's girl, but other times these women just want to be involved in everything, including your marriage.

He or She can't make it to kid functions

When your child is receiving a certificate for having good grades or perfect attendance or any award at all, you can't always count on your husband's or wife's attendance. Sometimes he/she is too busy at work; other times work is just an excuse. They are just not there because that small of a function may not be worth the time for them. Work it into your spouse's mind that these small celebrations only happen once, and it's best for everyone that both parents witness them.

Unknown Expectations

A relationship, especially a marriage, is made that much harder when you, or both of you, set unknown expectations of each other. If you expect him to help with dinner every Friday, you must tell him that, instead of assuming he knows what you want. You aren't a mind reader, and neither is he. So, if you have expectations, be sure that they are out in the open.

Not enough alone time

Once kids are in the mix, a lot of couples find it hard to spend enough alone time together. With so much emphasis put on having family time together and being a unit, sometimes the time set apart by you two to spend as husband and wife becomes a thing of the past. Remember, your time with your spouse is crucial if not more important now that you're married.

Too much time spent together

On the other hand, some couples spend too much time together. Even in a marriage, it's important that the two of you keep hold of your sense of self. Spending too much time together can cause you to feel trapped, or feel almost like you have no room to breathe. While you love your husband or wife, having time apart is ideal.

Sexual incompatibility

As crazy as it sounds, there comes a point in your marriage when the two of you become sexually incompatible. While some couples go into a marriage knowing that they aren't compatible in the bedroom, others see the issue manifest itself over time. Thankfully, sexual incompatibility can often be solved by a simple talk, with the two of you explaining what you like and dislike between the sheets, as well as any issues that you're having.

DEALING WITH SEX AND
WHEN IT GOES OUT THE WINDOW

You have become roommates. You eat together, watch television together, and go out, but you no longer have sex like you used to. You've probably heard tons of comments related to how sex seems to become a thing of the past once a couple gets married. Sex is very important in a marriage and should never be neglected. When does sex go out the window? Finance, kids, job, poor communication and arguments are factors that cause a bad physical relationship between couples. As a result, the relationship starts to wither away. Anyone of these issues can make having sex a little difficult and awkward in the relationship; it comes on then goes off. Men must remember that women are very sensitive and emotional. They are not like men; like a water fountain, they can turn their emotion on or off, when it comes to having sex the man's hormones can be stimulated no matter what kind of disagreement or argument that is going on. There are a lot of times a man would like to have sex; nothing else matters to him at this time, but for women, they are reluctant because their emotional needs to be met first. However, they can just go ahead and get it done quickly. Many wives are complaining that they're sexed out, they feel like they have had so much sex in their marriage and that they just don't want or need it anymore. This can only occur when sex is just a physical act. However, in marriage, sex was never designed to be "just physical." But unfortunately, people learn to separate the emotional and spiritual side of their sexuality, leaving just the physical; this often takes place years into the marriage. Healthy sex in marriage demands a physical, sexual, and emotional connection. Once a person turns off the emotions of sex, it's hard to turn it back on. They need to figure out what's causing the blockage and remove it, so they can get back to having great sex! Marriage doesn't have to mean the end of bedroom fun. However, it means you have a problem to solve.

Can couples in a marriage that has been sexless for months or years rekindle their sex lives again? Some do and some do not. If you have not had sex for a long time, it would be very hard to get it back. It is very important to talk about the sexless problem; if you do not talk about it, you cannot fix the problem. If you both sit down and come up with a solution for the problem, you should put 100% into making your sexless relationship work and become a strong sex relationship again. Be real to yourself and your spouse, do not be fake, because you would just be fooling yourself. Do things that will rekindle the desire. Examples are giving each other massages, going to the movies, going for walks or a getaway weekend trip. Do not try so hard to make it happen; just let it happen. Engage in some foreplay activities first, do not rush it. Take it nice and slow, enjoy being together. If you both really try, and it just won't work that doesn't mean you do not love each other, it means that you both just lost interest and do not have anything in common anymore. In my opinion, either you both decide to stay in a sexless marriage and be unhappy or go your separate ways and find someone else that will make you happy.

Ephesians 4:26 (KJV)

26 Be ye angry, and sin not: let not the sun go down on your wrath:

1 Corinthians 7:4 (KJV)

4 The wife hath not power of her own body, but the husband: and likewise also the husband hath not power of his own body, but the wife.

LOSING INTEREST IN EACH OTHER

Why do couples lose interest in each other after a few years of marriage? Because they have found out that married life is boring, and they no longer feel the pull of the power of attraction in that relationship. You lose the desire to observe the goodness of your spouse and drift apart in the relationship, and as a result, your relationship becomes stale and dull. You don't go anywhere anymore and you can't spend any money on yourselves, all you do is work, have kids and pay lots of bills. You both don't communicate like you used to, you can't sit down and talk anymore; you no longer eat together or make each other laugh anymore. You just don't enjoy being married and you've both lost interest. This happened because you lost touch of a simple thing. Oddly enough, at the beginning of the relationship, you knew that the simple things mattered but you ignored them.

Selfishness- Selfishness is possibly the most dangerous threat to a marriage. It affects how we talk with each other, how we divide responsibilities in the home, how we resolve conflicts, and even how we spend our time. Men and women most often ignore the needs of each other.

Galatians 5:26(KJV) - Let us not be desirous of vain glory, provoking one another, envying one another.

Disrespect- One of the main reasons marriages fail is that the husband or the wife does not seek of the best interest of the spouse. Especially if either spouse is disrespectful or dismissive about trying to repair issues in the marriage; this indicates that the one showing such disrespect no longer regards the other one as an equal partner. There is a significant difference between being angry or hurt with your spouse and treating them with scorn. Disrespect means you no longer value or cherish your spouse; this is a major problem in a relationship. Explain, if you'd like to fix the relationship, but when things are calm, express how hurt you feel when you are disrespected, and ask what triggers it.

1 Corinthians 7:3-5(KJV) -

3 *Let the husband render unto the wife due benevolence: and likewise also the wife unto the husband.*

4 *The wife hath not power of her own body, but the husband: and likewise also the husband hath not power of his own body, but the wife.*

5 *Defraud ye not one the other, except [it be] with consent for a time, that ye may give yourselves to fasting and prayer; and come together again, that Satan tempt you not for your incontinency.*

1 Corinthians 10:24 (KJV)

24 Let no man seek his own, but every man another's wealth.

Anger- If a husband and a wife are angry at each other a lot, it destroys the relationship. It makes it so painful that they want to get out of that relationship."

Psalms 37:8 Refrain from anger, and forsake wrath! Fret not yourself; it tends only to evil.

Galatians 5:19-21 Now the works of the flesh are evident: sexual immorality, impurity, sensuality, idolatry, sorcery, enmity, strife, jealousy, fits of anger, rivalries, dissensions, divisions, envy, drunkenness, orgies, and things like these. I warn you, as I warned you before, that those who do such things will not inherit the kingdom of God.

Separate Lives- is when couples stop spending enough time together. When a couple enters the covenant of marriage, the Bible tells us that God joins them together as one flesh.

Matthew 19:6 (KJV) 6 So then, they are no longer two but one flesh. Therefore what God has joined together, let not man separate."

Marriage is intended to be a lifelong commitment, not a temporary solution for loneliness or other emotional needs. God hates divorce and never intends for a couple to separate once they are married. Marriage vows should not be taken lightly, and separation should not be under-taken casually. Couples today decide to have a "trial separation" in order to discover what they truly want. But they do so without any attempt to rebuild the marriage during this time. Instead of rebuilding the family on a foundation of faith in Christ, they drift farther apart until they eventually divorce. This is not part of God's perfect plan for marriage and family, even if it has become acceptable in our culture. The woman you love through all the meaningless days of your life is the flesh of your flesh which that God has given you. The wife God gives a man is his reward, and the husband that God gives to the woman is her reward.

Communication- Words, they start out small but can grow into something big if you let it. It is a big problem when the emotional connection is lost and couples can no longer share opinions, and make attempts to resolve conflict. Many attempts to solve problems result in communication failure, especially when one person feels misunderstood. How many times do you react when a loved one doesn't understand you? We want to know that our husband or wife understands us, and when we don't feel understood, we react, whether silently, verbally, or with action. Usually, those reactions are negative, and they feed into it. It is estimated that when we're awake, we spend approximately 70% of our time communicating; 30% of which is talking. This means that over half of our communication is non-verbal. It's not what you say; it's how you say it, and that can be the singular cause of the communication problems between you and your spouse. If you say one thing for instance, such as "everything is good" but your body language says something else with a withdrawn face, it is obvious you communicated wrongly. Communicate successfully so that you can get what you need, and so that everyone involved is happy.

James 1:19 - Wherefore, my beloved brethren, let every man be swift to hear, slow to speak, slow to wrath:

Proverbs 15:1 - A soft answer turneth away wrath: but grievous words stir up anger.

Dishonesty – marriage is a partnership between a man and a woman. If lies, deceit, and disloyalty with secret habits become resident in the covenant, problems deepen. When a spouse discovers little lies and allows them to continue -- an equally destructive form of dishonesty; it reinforces his/her partner that lying is acceptable. Finding out why a person is lying is the first step to restoring trust. Being untruthful often signals insecurity, but it presents an opportunity for a married couple to explore what is really going on beneath the surface. However, sometimes lying deals a killer blow to a marriage. Cheating is the ultimate form of dishonesty, and marriages rarely recover from it. Even when a couple tries to move on, trust is shattered, and it is almost impossible to restore it enough to maintain a healthy relationship. Marriage counseling can help when lying is an issue, but even the best therapist cannot restore lost faith, except the couples are committed to work through it.

Colossians 3:9 - Lie not one to another, seeing that ye have put off the old man with his deeds;

Hebrews 13:18 - Pray for us: for we trust we have a good conscience, in all things willing to live honestly.

Not Feeling secure

A man is responsible for the environment and the direction of the relationship. After a man physically, emotionally, spiritually, mentally and financially leads, he is stressed. This might make him to argue with her; however, sometimes the argument might be because he does not know how to break down her barriers when she is upset. When this happens, she shuts down from him emotionally and physically, and then loses interest in sex. Your job as a man is to recognize when your woman shuts down, so you can open her back up to you through communication. Ask her what's wrong? Tell her she seems a little distant and that you want to know what's in her heart? Say things like, "tell me more and don't leave anything out," "I want to understand where you are coming from; what else is bothering you?" You will know when you've got to the root cause of the issue and have resolved it to her satisfaction. She will sigh in relief and probably say I feel so much better! I'm so glad we talked! Until you hear those words, you need to keep digging and getting her to talk about her emotions and her feelings without trying to solve the problem. For women talking about their problems makes them feel vulnerable. Examples of the thoughts that can stem their insecurity are "What if we don't have enough money to pay the mortgage or what if we lost our job or even worse, we got really sick?" "What if someone dies or didn't have life insurance," These are very real legitimate concerns, but unfortunately with such thoughts, insecurity comes in to play. She needs help to resolve and work through them. This can also cause them to question if God is really in control and if his hand protects over us all. Getting them to talk will also reveal if the issue has to do with the needs of the relationship, managing money, keeping your word or something you have done to hurt them.

Psalms 122:7 (KJV) Peace be within thy walls [and] prosperity within thy palaces.

Jeremiah 33:6 (KJV) Behold, I will bring it health and cure, and I will cure them, and will reveal unto them the abundance of peace and truth.

CHAPTER 5

DIDN'T SEE IT COMING

When you found out your spouse was having an affair and didn't see it coming. "My gut was telling me that things weren't quite right, but they had convinced me that I was just paranoid and insecure. I had no idea he was such a good liar. I made a list of unusual behaviors. I did not see anything different at that time. But looking back now, I see the signs that he was having an affair."

Here are a few signs:

1. About six months ago, he or she started working longer hours and having more excuses.
2. When he/she was home, they would seem restless and often claim they had work to do, so he spends a lot more time in his home office with the door closed.
3. He/she started talking about a person at work; how great the person is at their job. They would also tell you how funny the person is.
4. Him or her started to skip desserts and was very careful about what he or she ate (he lost weight and started exercising).
5. They seemed more short-tempered. Things that didn't usually bother them suddenly did, they became impatient, especially with the children.

I wish I'd been more alert. I just didn't put all the pieces together until it was too late. We should be more and learn these lessons to guard our marriages.

These warning signs may indicate an affair:

1. Changing eating and sleeping patterns;
2. Wearing a fresh style of clothes;
3. Starting arguments or becoming very passive;
4. Working longer or different hours;

5. Pulling away from the church and extended family;
6. Taking more showers than usual;
7. Comparing his or her spouse to other people;
8. Hiding credit card charges and cash withdrawals
9. Taking off his or her wedding ring.
10. Becoming secretive or defensive about phone calls and emails.

You don't need to be paranoid or to see things that aren't there. I don't recommend that you go sneaking around checking on your spouse, but if you need to, feel at ease. It would be wise, however, to be on guard.

Guard Yourself

Affairs begin in many ways and for many reasons, so you must always be on guard for the slightest hint of temptation. Because hints turn into flirtations, flirtations turn into attractions, attractions turn into affairs, and affairs turn into disasters. God will always provide a way of escape, but we must decide to run toward the door. When you're guarding your marriage, you're not guarding just your spouse, but yourself too.

1 Corinthians 10:13 (KJV)

13 No temptation has overtaken you except such as is common to man; but God is faithful, who will not allow you to be tempted beyond what you are able, but with the temptation will also make the way of escape, that you may be able to bear it.

1 Thessalonians 4:3-4 (KJV)

3 For this is the will of God, even your sanctification, that ye should abstain from fornication:

4 That every one of you should know how to possess his vessel in sanctification and honour;

WHEN CHEATING BEGINS

Cheating begins when you keep secret of your fantasies about another person from your companion. Furthermore, you increase this newly developed infatuation through calls; texts or emails or by hosting and meeting them in a secret location. The very moment you feel a tingle of excitement to get that correspondence and keep it to yourself, your cheating has begun.

It starts in the heart before manifesting physically. When I say the heart, I mean spiritually; your inner self; your soul. It starts when you start sneaking around and become secretive about things. You can't say the same thing you say to that person in private when your spouse is standing beside you.

Here are some signs of cheating.

1. Telling the untruth
2. Flirt with others
3. Engage in sexual talk with someone else.
4. Gossiping against husband/wife among friends.
5. Reveal any personal things about intimacy/sex life.

6. Having a sexual relationship with another man/ woman.
7. Exchange personal e-mails or text messages.

Everyone has got his or her own way of living life. Cheating may start from the following

1. Over Possessiveness.
2. Broken or incomplete relationships.
3. Over expectations.
4. Sexual Dissatisfaction
5. Loose friend circle.
6. Isolation from family.
7. Spending time with specific individuals.
8. Frustration.
9. Over-demanding attitudes.

Too often, we see this issue in a relationship. The best way to handle this situation is communication.

Facts and Statistics about Infidelity

Given the secretive nature of infidelity, exact figures about cheating and extra-marital affairs are nearly impossible to establish. It is estimated that roughly 30% to 60% of all married individuals in the United States will engage in infidelity at some point during their marriage, and  these numbers are probably on the conservative side. Because close to half of all marriages end in divorce, and Research consistently shows that 2% to 3% of all children are the product of infidelity. Most of these children are unknowingly raised by men who are not their biological fathers. DNA testing is finally making it easy for people to check the paternity of their children. Infidelity is becoming more common among people under 30. Many experts believe this increase in cheating is due to greater time spent away from their spouse. There are usually no signs of cheating because the person being cheated on was not looking to recognize the signs, not paying attention to the signs or just chose to ignore the signs. But, in hindsight, you will always find signs of infidelity. Men are more likely to cheat than women. But women are becoming more financially independent and are beginning to take on more men like traits when it comes to infidelity.

Wives and cheating husbands and why men and women cheat.

Unfortunately, many cheaters think they have found a more suitable replacement for their spouse. They believe the person they are cheating with is a more suitable person than their spouse. Although in some other cases, many people cheat because they have fantasies of being involved with someone other than their spouse.

You both will be tempted, but each of you must remember what they have at home. You should have love, compassion and respect for one another. A potential cheating situation begins when you are attracted to a man or a woman you approach. Always remember the covenant you've struck at home. You must always resist the temptation, remember the Bible says that the mission of the devil is to steal, kill and destroy. Your marriage is no exception; he came to steal your happiness and destroy your marriage. Do not get mad at the woman or the man who came in and tried to steal your spouse. You should get upset with your wife or husband because they should know what they have at home. So, if a woman is trying to seduce a married man, that man should be strong enough to walk away. On the other hand, if a man tries to seduce a married woman, she should be strong enough to walk away. State it sternly to the person that you have great value for your commitments at home and walk away. Mind your thoughts, I believe cheating begins when you have fantasies about a person

1 Corinthians 7:1-3 (KJV)

1 Now concerning the things whereof ye wrote unto me: It is good for a man not to touch a woman.

2 Nevertheless, to avoid fornication, let every man have his own wife, and let every woman have her own husband.

3 Let the husband render unto the wife due benevolence: and likewise, also the wife unto the husband.

UNHEALTHY RELATIONSHIPS

Bad relationships can take many forms and can be with a husband, wife, boyfriend, girlfriend or partner. How do you know if you're in an unhealthy relationship? The answers to these questions can help you figure it out:

1. In your relationship, do you usually feel happy and energized? Or do you often feel unhappy and drained?
2. After you spend time with the one you love, do you usually feel good or bad about yourself?
3. Do you feel physically and or emotionally safe with this person?
4. Is there equal give and take in the relationship or do you feel like you're always giving, and the other is always receiving?
5. When you are both having a conversation, does it lead to an argument?
6. Do you feel like you must always make the one you love happy in the relationships and not yourself?

Now check your answers to see what type of relationship you have:

Healthy relationships are characterized by compassion, security, safety, freedom of thinking, sharing, listening, mutual love and caring, healthy debates, disagreements, and respectfulness, especially when there are differences in opinions.

Unhealthy relationships are characterized by insecurity, abuse of power, control, selfishness, insecurity, self-centeredness, criticism, negativity, dishonesty, distrust, demeaning comments, attitudes, and jealousy.

Healthy relationships tend to leave you... feeling happy and energized. Unhealthy relationships tend to leave you feeling depressed and depleted.

Changing an Unhealthy Relationship

The first step to changing an unhealthy relationship is to recognize you're in one. Many people in unhealthy relationships are in denial, even though friends or family members have seen and told them of the danger signs.

The next step, equally as important, is to believe that you deserve to be treated with respect, love, and compassion. There are many reasons people stay in unhealthy relationships.

One common reason is an underlying low self-esteem that makes some people believe that they don›t deserve anything better. This kind of change in thinking, however, may not come easily and may require professional help from a counselor or a Pastor.

Unhealthy relationships do not only hurt psychologically; they can also be physically damaging.

An unhealthy relationship can exist among married couples, people who are dating and even those who are no longer a couple.

No matter the nature of the relationship, they have one thing in common; they are bad for your health.

RELATIONSHIPS CAN AFFECT YOUR HEALTH

Your boyfriend, girlfriend, or spouse can influence everything from sleep to blood pressure.

For better or worse and sickness and in health

Can your relationship status make a difference in your overall health condition? If you are really in a great relationship, it will help you to avoid certain illnesses. A healthy relationship will help you adopt healthier habits and even live longer. On the other hand, troubled relationships tend to breed stress and weaken the immune system.

So many issues can affect our health; it could be the behaviors we exhibit toward each other or the habits that we pass on to each other." So, whether you're dating casually, shacking up, or already married, keep in mind that relationships can affect, your health, body, romance, spirit, mind, will and emotions.

Weight gain

Commonly, couples let themselves go after breaking up, separating, getting a divorce, or even while they are married. Some couples tend to gain weight as they settle into marriage and sometimes lose weight when a marriage ends.

But the opposite happens quite often, as well: "A happy couple can motivate each other to stay healthy they may even go to the gym together, set goals, and feel responsible for each other." When couples do pack on the pounds, it may be an emotional issue or just negligence. It may as a result of dissatisfaction in the relationship, hence the aggressive eating behaviors and sleep problems, which leads to weight gain, and other health issues.

Stress levels

In 2012 a survey was done by the American Psychological Association on stress in America. The survey shows that the top stress levels in a relationship are money, work, and economy. These stress levels can affect home life, intimacy, health and other areas in the relationship.

I believe that couples should have regular physical intimacy, this appears to reduce stress and boost a health condition. People who have healthy relationships have sex more frequently, and the report shows that they have greater satisfaction with their relationship and life overall.

Sex is just one part of a relationship. However, the way couples behave outside the bedroom can just as easily send stress levels soaring in the opposite direction. Couple disputes, disagreements over money, or even questions as simple as who works the most, due to the up and down economy have been shown to increase stress.

Significantly higher percentages of adult's report that stress impacts their physical and mental health. Symptoms such as headaches or feeling anxious have been experienced by 42 percent of adults. Depression has been reported by 37 percent and constant worrying by 33 percent in a substantial number of individuals in a 2014 report. These changes affect their behavior causing them to ignore their responsibilities and argue with their loved ones. One-quarter (25 percent) of those employed report snapping at or being short with co-workers because of stress. Health also becomes compromised in a relationship when stress is a factor.

(Statics retrieved from the American Psychological Association)

Sleep problems

Sleeping next to someone you love, and trust can help you fully relax and sleep better. And if your Relationship is bad, it can affect sleep in many ways. Relationship insecurity or conflict is associated with poor sleep, and to make matters worse, sleep problems can exacerbate relationship problems, creating a bad atmosphere. **According to a 2012 survey done by the American Psychological Association, "stress in America." Stress keeps more than 40 percent of adults awake at night.**

Lack of sleep causes health conditions like:

- Impulsive behavior
- Lack of focus
- Tiredness and irritation
- Difficulty in concentrating and making decisions
- Lack of Sex Drive

(Statics come from American Psychological Association)

Depression

Depression and anxiety often go hand in hand, so it makes sense that relationships can affect depression in similar ways. On the one hand, long-term relationships and marriages specifically can ease symptoms in people with a history of depression.

On the other hand, relationships that are dramatic, increase the risk of depression. Women, regardless of their personal and family history of depression, are more likely to be depressed if their husbands have been unfaithful, or if their marriages are falling apart. **Depression** is more than just sadness. People with depression may experience a lack of interest and pleasure in daily activities, significant weight loss or gain, insomnia or excessive sleeping, lack of energy, inability to concentrate, feelings of worthlessness or excessive guilt and recurrent thoughts of death or suicide. Depression is the most common mental disorder. Fortunately, depression is treatable.

(Statics come from American Psychological Association)

Alcohol use

Bad relationships can make a boyfriend, girlfriend, or spouse drink a lot more than normal. The impact on how much alcohol they consume, and how often they indulge in the act, can add more pressure in the marriage. Too much drinking, sometimes, tends to destroy a relationship. Drugs can also have the same impact.

It's also true that relationship conflict and a lack of intimacy can drive a boyfriend, girlfriend, or spouse to alcoholism. Both men and women drink more as a response to relationship problems, and excessive drinking can escalate those problems.

Here are just a few examples of how alcoholism negatively impacts relationships:

- Alcohol causes unnecessary arguments
- Violence
- Marital conflict
- Infidelity
- Jealousy
- Economic insecurity
- Divorce
- Fatal alcohol effect

If alcoholism has ruined your relationship. I urge you to get medical help or counseling to cure your drinking problem. If you love you, spouse and family, do this ASAP; get help.

Blood pressure

Your diet, exercise, and stress levels all have an impact on your blood pressure, so it's not a coincidence that your relationship status and the strength of your relationship can influence it.

Individuals in happy marriages tend to have a lower blood pressure than singles. People who are unhappily married, however, have the highest blood pressure readings.

Being in an unhealthy relationship causes your body to release stress hormones and your heart to beat faster; this can push your blood pressure up, over time. Always take out a moment, relax, and take deep breaths. Do not let anyone get your blood pressure up and out of control. Learn to take care of yourself.

Here are some ways to relax:

- Walking
- Breathing Exercises
- Eat Potatoes
- Watch Your Salt
- Chocolate
- Cut the Caffeine
- Lose weight

You can also practice deep meditation to lower your blood pressure. Below is the process. Close your mouth and eyes, sit down in a recliner chair or lay down on a couch. Relax and clear your mind, meditate, just relax and do nothing else.

Lowered Libido

When stress spikes, sex drive often suffers. This is because stress can make it very difficult for a man or woman to become sexually aroused. In effect, feeling overwhelmed and anxious about life causes our brains to prioritize certain activities over sex and that leaves little room for desiring and having great sex.

Heart health

Although everyone experiences stress in unusual ways, certain relationship situations are more likely to set the stage for chronic stress; examples are struggling to balance work and family, living in an unhappy marriage, and going through a divorce.

If healthy, the heart's valves open and close, precisely as the heart pumps blood throughout our bodies, and allow the flow of blood in only one direction. Heart valve disease occurs when the heart's valves are not working as they should, preventing the correct flow of blood and circulation to the body. Heart valve problems can be life-threatening, and they are one of the leading causes of congestive heart failure.

Pay Attention to your overall health

Although it might seem like nagging at times, if your boyfriend, girlfriend, or spouse convinces you that you have certain symptoms, make sure you take the prescribed medication

People in healthy relationships care for each other's health and feel obligated to take care of themselves too.

Healthy eating involves taking control of how much and what types of food you eat.

Let your body get a lot of rest

This allows you to take charge of your life and feel good about the choices you have made.

It allows you to gain energy (recharge), feel good, and keep fit.

When two people are married, they have made a vow of "in sickness and in death," and they should honor this vow.

Each spouse should make sure the other is fit and in good health. Yes, this may seem like they're nagging, but it's for your own good and it shows how much he/she cares.

When it comes to stress management and taking care of our health, 47 percent of adults engage in active methods, such as exercising or walking, meditation or yoga, and playing sports. When it comes to the services of psychologists, nearly half of adults have positive regard for the psychologist's ability to help manage stress. 45 percent say they think a psychologist can help a great deal.

(Statics come from American Psychological Association)

Heartache

It's not just your current relationship that can affect your health, your past ones can as well, especially those that ended up with hurt feelings and rejection. Thinking about an ex-lover can have similar effects on the brain as physical pain.

It's even possible for a breakup to result in something called a broken heart syndrome; a temporary enlargement of the heart with symptoms like a heart attack brought on by extreme physical or emotional stress. Women are most likely to experience the syndrome; though it can also show up in men as well.

This is how you get over past relationships and let go of past hurts

- Express your pain and responsibility.
- Decide to let it go.
- Don't maintain an intimate relationship with your ex.
- **Remove their photographs, gifts and love letters.**
- Focus on the present.
- Forgive them and yourself.
- Accept that the relationship has come to an end.
- Don't stalk or make plans for revenge.
- Take time to process the pain.
- And whatever you do, do not call or text.

Almost everyone will experience the break-up of a romantic relationship at some point in their lives, and unfortunately, most will likely experience break-ups several times during the course of their lives. Break-up or divorce can initially result from negative outcomes such as depression, loneliness, distress, and a loss of self-worth or a loss sense of who you are as a person. If you do not have a civil relationship or a friendship, the best solution is to stay apart from each other. If you have kids with each other, you must try to put your difference aside for your kids. You should not be selfish; thinking just about yourself, if the relationship is not working. If he or she keeps convincing you to come back every time you have a fight or other problems, make sure you do not get back with that person. You need to change your pattern because the other person knows your weakness. Do not let them manipulate the situation if you do not change, you would be like a revolving door, constantly in the same cycle. Do not let them control your life; take back control of your life.

CHAPTER 6

HOW TO SAVE YOUR MARRIAGE

Many couples come to me for help to save their marriages. In these cases, one of the couples is pushing for separation or divorce. The spouse who is asking for help wants to prevent separation or divorce. The spouse who wants to keep the marriage might have had no clue that things were that bad. In some cases, the party willing to save the marriage recognized that things were that bad but were willing to put up with the tough situation because of the mental health of the children. Whenever a marriage completely crashes, it is often because both parties have issues that need to be dealt with. This is why marriage counseling is very important. One spouse receiving marriage counseling will likely only result in a short-term solution because both partners would need counseling to figure out a way to mend the relationship. Sometimes, simply listening to the other person can help you understand what is wrong with the relationship, and you may even hear some recommendations on how to save your marriage from divorce. A breakdown in communication and finance is often the root cause of relationship problems, so repairing it can be beneficial when learning how to save a marriage. Listen to that person; also, be open to understanding how they are feeling; this may change the outcome of the relationship with all the problems laid out on the table. In addition to listening to your spouse's feelings, you also need to be able to express your own feelings, so that your spouse can understand your point of view. It is never an easy thing to express frustrations and difficulties with the person you love most dearly, so having a marriage counselor who can mediate and help in this discussion, can give you the motivation to speak your mind while keeping the discourse civil. You should never disrespect or put down your spouse because that will just create further animosity and resentment.

Marriage counseling is designed for couples to work through the problems they are having. With regards to several factors, this is one of the ways to save a marriage. Listening and then sharing your feelings can help address some of the problems, and marriage counseling is a wonderful place to do this. The marriage counselor guides the discussion between the couples and ensures they are both heard by themselves. Depending on the current state of the relationship, spend some time apart might be appropriate, so the couple can organize their thoughts and feelings.

Most spouses don't realize that taking a break in a relationship can be exactly what is needed when thinking of how to save a marriage. If the marriage has been stressful for quite some time, spending some time away from each other can only help the relationship. What would you be willing to change to save your marriage? Give your spouse time and space to think about it. After taking some time apart, you or your spouse may realize what it feels like to be without each other; this could be the perfect motivation for the both of you to give the marriage another shot. You must learn to forgive and forget. One thing that can bring a relationship down is holding on to the past. It is wrong to treat your spouse in that manner because they made mistakes that hurt you. Everyone makes mistakes; however, learning to forgive those wrongs will be great for the relationship; this is another lesson for saving a marriage. It isn't useful or helpful to dig up the past whenever your spouse does something that upsets you. Giving your spouse a clean slate, each day, will help your marriage to grow. Nobody likes being reminded of their past, whether it is real or fake, and your spouse is no different. Learning to forgive and forget can help to restore balance to your marriage. Saving a marriage also depends on the apology of your spouse. In an ideal world, both people in a relationship are meant to ask for forgiveness from each other. But even if this doesn't occur, it is still important to let go of past mistakes for the sake of the future of your relationship. For instance, never bring up in conversation past wrongs, you may think about it, but do not bring those issues up again. Although you will never forget, don't bring that issue up in a conversation with your spouse again. If the spouse does the same thing again, you have the right to bring it up again, but only for reference. This is the only time you are permitted to do this because your spouse repeated the same thing; otherwise it is history and should remain in the past.

1. Listen to your Spouse and don't ignore them
2. Express your Feelings and Concerns

3. Take responsibility for your Actions and be Willing to Compromise
4. Stop Blaming the Other Person for your Mistake(s)
5. Spend Some Time Apart if Necessary
6. Learn to Forgive and Forget
7. Find Some Common Goals

GETTING ADVICE

Pre-marriage Counseling
Pastor/ Marriage counselor

Pre-marriage counseling is a promising idea before you get married. So many problems can be sorted out before you both commit yourself to the marriage, including

- Argument
- General communication problems
- Issues with in-laws or friends
- Financial problems
- Problems with the children (if it's not your first marriage)
- Sexual problems

It may feel difficult to get the relationship you want because it seems so much is against you. You might even feel it's impossible to stop the marriage preparations. You have thought of telling your future wife or husband that you're worried and scared if you both don't resolve these issues before getting married, but you don't. In secret, you wonder if you should go ahead with it all.

The good news is that you could perhaps consider talking to your partner about making a positive step. You're much more likely to get a positive answer if you say you want to invest in the marriage by going for pre-marriage counseling.

If you're both committed to sorting things out, there's every chance that you can have the relationship and marriage you want. A couple/ marriage counselor can certainly help you on your way.

Even if you're planning on getting a divorce, get advice from your pastor or a marriage counselor, pray about it and find a good counselor. Find two

people that you can confide in and discuss your problems with them.

Do not tell everyone about your problems because everyone does not want to see you happy.

What is missing in your marriage? I have written some questions down, check the circles that you feel can help your marriage so that we all can have a strong marriage.

- **Acceptance** -Nobody is perfect. We all have our weaknesses and flaws. Accept your spouse for who he or she really is, and do not try to change each other.
- **Affection** – This is important for couples can be one of the first things to go after children are born or when a marriage is in trouble.
- **Commitment** – you feel that your husband or wife is fully committed to the marriage.
- **Communication** – couples do not know how to talk to each other in some marriages, this can lead to divorce. Beware of the signs that indicate that you both are becoming strangers
- **Compassion** -Couples should be sensitive to each other's feelings, and they should also be ready to console and support one another in times of pain, problems, and difficulties.
- **Disappointed** – in some cases, when couples become disappointed in their marriage, the disappointment might be about something they may not be getting from their spouse; it could be emotional connectedness, an affirmation of some kind, or physical closeness.
- **Discouraged** - Husband and wife are trying to resolve their issues but they are setting themselves up for feelings of discouragement in marriage. Nothing is going the right way.
- **Encouragement** -Couples should learn to encourage each other to go for the things that make them happy. They should be able to lift each other up in times when they need it the most.
- **Gifts** -lack of gift-giving is very discouraging if neither one will buy a gift for the other. Sometimes gifts show how much you love one another.

- **Honesty** -Couples should be able to talk about anything with their partner. Being honest about how you feel about every situation will help you both resolve every issue you have to face.
- **Insecurities** - today couples are very concerned about insecurities. Insecurity is a feeling of uncertainty, a lack of confidence or anxiety about yourself. Insecurity becomes present in a relationship when irrational thoughts and fears that you are not good enough, that you will not be ok without a husband or wife, that you will never find anyone better, that you are not truly lovable, emerge.
- **Listen** -some couples have poor listening skills; they choose to listen and hear what they want to hear; this usually causes a strain on the relationship. Not listening correctly, and not doing what he or she asks will put additional strain on the relationship.
- **Loyalty** -Couples should be loyal to one another and not do anything to destroy the promise they made before God.
- **Love** - Love has nothing to do with how you feel. Love is a command given to us by God. Love is a decision that requires unconditional commitment.

1 Corinthians 13:4-7 (NIV)

4 Love is patient, love is kind. It does not envy, it does not boast, it is not proud. 5 It does not dishonor others, it is not self-seeking, it is not easily angered, it keeps no record of wrongs. 6 Love does not delight in evil but rejoices with the truth. 7 It always protects, always trusts, always hopes, always perseveres.

- **Passionate** - How do you stir up and keep the passion alive? It starts with desire. You must want it. You must be careful about going after a passionate, intimate marriage, and be willing to do whatever it takes to reach that goal and keep it. Engaging your heart fully in the joyful pursuit of a passionate marriage is the first step toward attaining it.
- **Patience** -In times of misunderstandings and shortcomings, couples should not let anger and frustration overcome them. Instead, they should be patient with each other, focusing on resolving the issues together.

- **Respect** -the couple should always treat each other with respect to show how much they value one another.
- **Romantic** - The strength of your marriage depends on the choices you make to improve it. I'm convinced that the lack of dating and romance in marriage is one of the major causes of broken relationships. Marriages usually don't break up overnight. They collapse because they lack daily deposits of love, communication, and affirmation.
- **Security** - creates a strong foundation for financial security, leading to a healthy marriage that will last 'til death does you part. Plus, you'll be stopping money fights before they even start. Now while still being able to cover emergencies and future financial goals, imagine not having to worry about paying your bills or buying a car because you have the cash to buy without taking on new debt! That peace of mind means you're financially secure and this makes your marriage stronger.
- **Support** – couples should support one another in their ideas; like starting Ministries or going back to school etcetera. That is what marriage is all about; working together
- **Temper** - A person married to someone with a bad temper often feel like they walk around on eggshells. They may feel like they can't disagree with their Husband or wife and may try hard to make things as peaceful as possible. This is a stressful way to live, if you feel like you can't express your true feelings to your Husband or wife, that is a problem.
- **Time** -married couples need to make more time for each other. They can go out for dinner, catch a movie, etc. Better yet, discover new things to do together whether it's a night or a weekend plan, inscribe the date and time on your calendar, put it in your computer planner, or enter it on your phones to do list.
- **Trust** - When you trust your significant other, you will feel free to share your heart and soul with him or her, because you know what you share will be valued. Trust provides the means for your relationship to build a stronger platform upon which you can weather life's ups and downs together. Lack of trust can lead to a lot of pain, misunderstandings, arguments, and stress.

Whether you agree or disagree with the words I picked out above, it will help you to question your own marriage. Maybe you and your spouse are wanting the same thing, but you both are not sure how to get there together, understanding what makes the ideal marriage is a key to help you on this journey.

CONCLUSION

It sounds romantic to love someone with all your heart and soul whether or not they love you back. But the reality is very different the pain of loving someone who doesn't feel the same way about you can be almost unbearable it certainly doesn't feel romantic. It just feels devastating people can wear pain on the outside like a mask, hiding them from the world but it also can hide deep within them waiting to be freed by some emotional circumstance. Your relationship isn't doomed just because you think it's one-sided. The most important thing is that your relationship works for you. I've observed many relationships from the outside that seem one-sided, but internally sometime both partners feel good about what the other one is bringing to the relationship. Love is a gift from God to you so you can share your love with the one you chose to be with. If you do not know how to use the gift of love it will be taken from you. I believe love is a priceless diamond because a diamond has thousands of reflections, and each reflection represents love you can accept a person's imperfections without any condition and able to transfer the love I have to give to another person who I am attracted to. With love I can have the power against loneliness, sadness, and illness, and to be able to change this into my happiness love or to be loved. And it's not fair to be hurt by someone to whom you have invested so much love and time it's not fair to give all your trust to someone that might betray you in the end.

NOTES

NOTES

NOTES

NOTES

NOTES

NOTES

Made in the USA
Monee, IL
03 February 2021

58490366R00059